Redistribution

A Silent Counter-Revolution?

By Michael Barratt Brown

Michael Barratt Brown was the founding Principal of Northern College. He is the author of Defending the Welfare State (Spokesman Books, £6.99).

The last two decades have seen a counter-revolutionary shift in power and wealth.

Political revolutions are about rapid changes in the relations of power in an organisation, most particularly in a nation state or among nation states. Counter-revolutions reverse the process with similar speed. As the result of some sudden fundamental change, generally associated with violence, power is concentrated in different hands, and in a changed power structure. It can well be argued that in this sense there was a revolution during and immediately after the Second World War. The wealth of the rich was curtailed and the position of the poor enhanced – in advanced industrial countries and between them and the one-time colonies. Everyone knew it was happening. In the last twenty years, however, we can now recognise that there has occurred a counter-revolution in the advanced countries, including the United Kingdom, and equally in their relations with the developing countries throughout the whole world.

In the main, this counter-revolution has been without violence, and I have called it 'silent' because it has not been trumpeted aloud. There have been acts of violence in the United Kingdom – during the miners' strike, in Ireland, and in repressive laws. World-wide, there have been wars – most particularly the Cold War and the arms race, followed by wars in the Gulf, in former Yugoslavia, in Chechnya, in Palestine, in Afghanistan and now, again, in Iraq. This list of wars in the last two decades does not include continued fighting in much of Africa, in parts of Latin America, in Indonesia, in Kashmir and Sri Lanka, where the power structure has been questioned. The main open challenge has come from those Arabs and Muslims who sense that it is their religion and ethnicity, as well as their share of the world's wealth, that is being threatened.

AF875204

For most people living in the United Kingdom, in much of Europe, in North America and some other parts of the world, there is little sense that there has been a revolution or counter-revolution, certainly not a violent one. The collapse of the Soviet Union was sudden and total, but not violent. Most of the changes elsewhere seem to have crept up on us silently. They are nonetheless considerable.

In international relations most people are aware of the fundamental nature of the change in power – those who hold it and the structure of power. Yet even the fall of the Soviet Union is not seen as a revolutionary change. The Soviet Union simply collapsed, in part the result of the arms race. There was no military victory, but the effects were certainly counter-revolutionary. Now there is only one world superpower – the United States – and people are becoming aware that United States governments (Democrat or Republican) have the clear aim of what they call 'full spectrum dominance', i.e. in space and on land, sea and air, including the stratosphere and telecommunication.

The full implications of this new counter-revolution are not clearly understood, though the statements about unilateral pre-emptive strikes made by President Bush are beginning to make them clearer. Commentators such as Martin Wolf of the *Financial Times* have argued (*Prospect*, February 2003, p.73), that world-wide inequalities have been reduced. This argument can only be sustained by taking figures for the decade of the 1990s. In this decade some improvements, especially in China and East Asia, did something to offset the sharply widening inequality of the previous two decades, but not enough to check the long-term trend. It is also necessary for this argument to assume that the situation will not worsen in the world economic recession of the first decade of the new century.

Most people would accept, from what is said by governments and in the media of press, radio and television, that the gap between rich and poor countries world-wide has been widening as the power of capital, and especially of American capital, has grown. What is less well understood is the simultaneous change in power relations *inside* the nation states. The change has been great, but it has hardly been resisted. Books such as George Monbiot's *The Captive State* (Macmillan 2000) and his articles on the take-over of Britain by capital, which are published in *The Guardian*, let alone the publications of the remaining left-wing press, have only a narrow circulation. The same is true of similar books written in Europe, such as those by Pierre Bourdieu, or in the USA, like those of Gabriel Kolko. Yet they describe a shift in power in Britain, in Europe, in the United States and inside nations elsewhere that can only be described as revolutionary. Mr Blair's spin doctors heralded New Labour in 1996 as 'The Blair Revolution', but even those who challenged this at the time, as Ken Coates and I did (in *The Blair Revelation*, Spokesman 1996) scarcely envisaged the scale of the counter-revolution.

How much of a counter-revolution?

In what then does this counter-revolution consist? Fundamentally it involves an immense strengthening of the power of capital and weakening of the power of labour. In essence, the strength of capital in a capitalist system arises from the unequal distribution of capital, and the built-in pressure for capital accumulation of competing capitals. This strength is only offset by the resistance of organised labour, with the support of state regulation, combined with the system of taxes and benefits which trade union and other popular pressures have built up into what we call the 'Welfare State'.

In the United States, however, both the two main political parties represent capital; and labour has little political power or economic power, although there is a surviving tradition of democratic rights. The trade unions are weak and the labour force is deeply divided by colour and ethnic origin. In Europe, some countries have strong trade unions, but nearly all political parties have, since the Second World War, been committed to the concept of a contract between labour and capital as the basis of citizenship in the nation state. In the United Kingdom, where there was no such contractual concept, labour through its trade unions has succeeded by past struggles in achieving a recognised place in a society where the people are still subjects of royal prerogative, albeit exercised together with an elected prime minister.

In the last twenty years, however, there have been fundamental changes in this balance of power. All the European social democratic parties have moved to the right, whether they are in government or in opposition, increasingly embracing the aims and interests of capitalist business. Since the collapse of the Soviet Union, European capital has felt free to operate without fear of driving labour into the hands of the Communists. The emergence of 'fat cats' in industry and services is only one manifestation of a much deeper development. The whole concept in most European countries of a contract between labour and capital is being eroded. In the United Kingdom in the last twenty years, the power of the unions has been very greatly diminished, after fifty years of enhancement. All three main political parties in the United Kingdom now claim to be parties of business. Against this a Socialist Alliance in England fields candidates, but has not yet found the means to appeal to a mass electorate. Socialists in Scotland have done better, and both Sinn Fein and Plaid Cymru have a socialist as well as a nationalist element.

The position of organised labour throughout the United Kingdom has been degraded by the decline of the unions' base in mining and manufacturing as a result of industrial collapse in face of foreign competition, by Tory legislation against trade union power, which New Labour has not repealed, and by the introduction of flexible labour practices and part-time in place of full-time employment. Trade unions have about half the number of members that they once had and their influence on a Labour government, which was once decisive, is virtually nil. Even a large vote at the 2002 Labour Party Conference against privatising public services was shrugged off by the government. New Labour is dominated at all levels of government by the representatives of large-scale capital. My booklet *The Captive Party* (Spokesman, 2001) gave the details.

The public sector and the associated Welfare State, once the crowning achievement of years of labour struggle, are being steadily undermined by privatisation. This did not happen suddenly or violently, but it is nonetheless a counter-revolution. It is only necessary to remember that little more than 20 years ago a Labour cabinet minister and serious claimant to the leadership of the Labour Party (Tony Benn) proclaimed that he stood for 'making an irreversible shift in power and wealth to working people and their families.' How have the mighty fallen!

I have called this a silent revolution, although it has been engineered fairly deliberately by owners of capital and by governments seeking to appease them. That governments have moved this way has been the result of three main factors: the collapse of the Soviet Union and with it the erosion of belief in an alternative to the power of capital; the relatively high standard of living of the great majority of the people in the advanced industrial countries, especially the increase in home ownership; and, finally, the absence of claims, the Mandelson-Liddle spin-book on *The Blair Revolution* apart, that there was anything revolutionary in progress. This absence was, of course, quite deliberate, just one aspect of spin doctoring and the concealment of what is actually happening which has become typical of modern government.

In political parlance today, words are highjacked to give a contrary meaning. When Mr Blair insists on 'reform' in the social services, in health and education and in government, it is a counter-reformation that he has in mind, and on which he is engaged – going back on social provision for all in the state pension, the National Health Service, comprehensive schooling. Rhetoric about giving people choice and individual freedom and challenging vested interests provides a cover for the exclusion of popular representation, the destruction of local institutions and the centralisation of power. Mrs Thatcher showed the way, and New Labour has followed. Taxes on the rich were reduced, while state spending was just about maintained, by the simple, but once for all, expedient of selling the family silver, disposing of the public sector – at knock-down prices to private buyers. And New Labour has been happy to continue the sales. So, step by step, people have found that they are in a new world – of falling pensions, of fat cats, a third of our children in poverty, and the threat of unemployment looming. What is evident is that this realisation, though it has come surprisingly late, has at length come into the general public consciousness.

It has for long seemed hard to believe that the post-war world of the second half of the 20th Century was ended – a time of peace and full employment and the prospect of steady improvement, in living standards, in health and housing, and in wider educational opportunities for all. But, as the reality is recognised for what it is – the threat of global war, the declining worth of pensions, an impoverished health service, an educational crisis, unsafe and unreliable railways, gridlock and pollution in the cities, disease on the farms, rising crime and hooliganism in the cities and growing general inequality of incomes – the rich getting richer and the poor getting poorer – there must come a revulsion. But the counter-revolution has already taken place and it will not be easy to challenge, the change has been so great. Redistribution, which has been working in reverse to enrich the rich and impoverish the poor, will not so easily be put back into positive mode – to the benefit of the poor.

Redistribution – to the rich

Let those who doubt the scale and effects of this counter-revolution ponder the change in the shares of rich and poor in total United Kingdom household post-tax incomes over the years from 1978 to 2002, as they are revealed by official statistics on 'The effects of taxes and benefits on household incomes' shown in Table I. The bottom fifth (quintile) of households who once had 10% of all such incomes have had this reduced to 6%. Even the next three quintiles up the scale have lost shares. Only the top fifth have gained over these years, their share rising by a massive ten points from 36% to 46%. The only effect that New Labour has had since 1997 has been to further widen the gap between rich and poor.

The Table shows the distribution of incomes at four stages between five income groups, each amounting to one fifth of the total households – a quintile – according to their share of the total. The first stage is original income before benefits and different kinds of taxes are counted in. The second shows gross income, the result of adding in cash benefits like pensions and income support. The third is disposable income after deducting direct taxation (that is income tax and national insurance contributions). The fourth is post tax income after indirect taxation like VAT is deducted. This structure constitutes the intervention of the Welfare State, which supposedly redistributes incomes from the rich to the poor.

The balance of power of capital and labour establishes the distribution of original incomes, full employment providing the most favourable circumstances for the mass of households without capital and thus raising the share of the poorer. Full employment in the 1960s and 70s did much to raise the share of original income of the lower half of the households. Their shares fell sharply under the

TABLE I

INEQUALITY: NEW LABOUR'S FIVE YEARS, OLD LABOUR AND THE TORY RECORDS

Percentage Shares of All Household Incomes Selected Years 1978-2001-2

Income groups (quintiles)	1978 Lab.	1980 Tory	1988 Tory	1996-7 Tory	1997-8 N-Lab.	1998-9 N-Lab.	1999-01 N-Lab.	2001-2 N-Lab
Original Income								
Bottom	3	2	2	2	2	3	2	3
2nd	10	9	7	7	7	7	7	7
3rd	18	18	16	15	15	15	15	14
4th	26	26	26	25	25	25	25	24
Top	43	44	50	51	51	52	51	52
	100	100	100	100	100	100	100	100
Gross Income								
Bottom	9	8	7	7	7	7	6	6
2nd	13	13	11	11	11	11	11	11
3rd	18	18	16	16	16	16	16	15
4th	23	23	23	23	23	23	23	22
Top	37	38	43	44	44	44	44	45
	100	100	100	100	100	100	100	100
Disposable Income								
Bottom	10	9	8	8	8	7	7	7
2nd	14	13	11	12	12	12	12	12
3rd	18	18	16	16	16	16	16	16
4th	23	23	23	23	23	23	23	22
Top	35	37	42	42	42	42	42	43
	100	100	100	100	100	100	100	100
Post-tax Income								
Bottom	10	9	7	7	7	6	6	6
2nd	14	13	11	11	11	11	11	11
3rd	18	17	16	16	16	16	16	15
4th	23	23	22	22	22	22	22	22
Top	36	38	44	44	44	45	45	46
	100	100	100	100	100	100	100	100

Notes to Table I: Figures do not necessarily add up to 100 because of rounding
Original income = before government intervention
Gross income = including cash benefits (pensions etc.)
Disposable income = minus direct taxes, national insurance
Post-tax income = after indirect taxes (VAT etc.)
These figures do NOT include benefits in kind (health, education etc.)

Source: 'The effects of taxes and benefits on household incomes', *Economic Trends*, May 2003, page 70, Table 26

Tories, and recent full employment including women's increased part-time employment has not improved their shares, although the very poorest have seen a very slight improvement from 2% to 3%. All the others in the lower groups have fared no better under New Labour than under the Tories when their combined share went down from 28% to 22%. It fell to 21% at the last count. Only the top group has continued to benefit, enjoying now a record 52% of all original income, compared with 43% in 1978.

The most obvious change, then, since 1978 has been in the rise of the fat cats. A survey in 2002 (reported in *The Independent*, 28.07.02) published by the Halifax showed that executives in large companies had enjoyed a rise in their incomes over the decade of the 1990s of 110%, compared with an average rise in wages of 45%. By contrast, teachers, nurses, firefighters and police officers all received less than the average figure. The lowest paid workers were found to be in child care. Richard Towers, director of the Low Pay Unit, is quoted by *The Independent* as saying that the Government could do more to reduce inequalities by improving pay for front line public sector staff, and he goes on:

'We have the strange notion that to get the rich to work harder we pay them more and to get the poor to work harder you pay them less. The quality of a service is not determined by the managers at the top, it is determined by people who actually deliver it. I think in most places you would notice if the cleaners stopped coming in long before you noticed that the senior managers stopped turning up.' (*Health Which?* reported in October 2002 that there were 26,280 managers in the NHS, almost as many as the 30,000 GPs including part-timers and locums). The Government says it does not want all the money it puts into public services disappearing in pay, 'but', Towers asks, 'how are improvements going to be delivered except through people? If those people are underpaid and demoralised then it is not going to improve.'

What happened to the Welfare State?

Apart from the growing inequalities in original income, what is equally obvious from Table I is that the Welfare State has done nothing to offset this process. When we look at gross income, that is after counting in cash benefits, mainly pensions and income support, there is a marked increase in the shares of the lower groups compared with shares of original income, but compared with what they had in the 1970s the three lowest groups have only 32% compared with their earlier 40%. The lowest quintile is actually worse off under New Labour, with 6% of the total compared with 7% under the Tories and with 9% in 1978. The other two lower groups are also worse off than they were, with 26% of the total compared with 31% in 1978. Again it is the top group that has been the one to gain, raising its share from 37% to 45%. The other, poorer groups have seen no change in their shares under New Labour, but they still have only 28% compared with 32% in 1978.

The Welfare State was intended not only to make up for low incomes, but to do so by taxing the higher incomes. Yet since the 1970s, direct taxation, that is income tax and national insurance, has hardly helped. After direct taxes are paid, the poorest group has 7% today, well below the 10% in 1978, and this is even worse under New Labour than the 8% under the Tories. Again the richest group has gained under New Labour with 43% compared with 42% under the Tories, compared with only 35% under 'old' Labour in 1978.

When we come finally to income shares after indirect taxes like VAT are allowed for, that is in post-tax income, the shares are roughly back to where they were in gross income, with the richest group gaining a point under New Labour. Far from redistributing in favour of the poor, between 1978 and the years 1998-2002, the richest fifth gained 8 to 9 points in their share of original income, but gained 9 to 10 points in post tax income. The poorest fifth had the same share of original income, but as much as four points less of post-tax income. In considering the several stages revealed in the Table, cash benefits, mainly pensions, do continue to add substantially to original income to make up the gross income for the two lowest groups. But these additions are considerably less today than 24 years ago, bringing the very poorest group up from a share in total gross incomes of 3% to 6%, instead of from 3% to 10% as in 1978. That the additions are still as large is the result of the increase in the numbers of those drawing pensions. Not surprisingly the pension system has been the object of fierce criticism from richer tax payers, to which New Labour has been responding positively.

We may sum up the working of the Welfare State today from what the Table has shown. When taxes are taken into account, both indirect (VAT etc.) and direct (income tax and national insurance), *the tax system has practically no effect on the final distribution of incomes after taxation,* leaving the share of the total received by the poorest fifth of households still at 6% after cash benefits are received and taxes are paid, and the richest fifth slightly better off with 46%, and the middle groups with exactly the same shares of post-tax income as they had of gross income. Direct taxes on incomes and national insurance payments had served to reduce the gap very slightly to 7% for the poorest and 43% for the richest. But this was then reversed after all taxes were paid by the impact of indirect taxes, back to respectively 6% for the poorest and 46% for the richest, while the other intermediate groups had their shares largely unchanged. The report in *Economic Trends* does also show some figures for the poorest and richest tenth of the households in 2001-2. *The poorest tenth received 1% and the richest tenth 34% of original income, and respectively 2% and 31% of post-tax income.* Big deal!

The UK tax system is now in its effect regressive. The rich may pay more in taxes absolutely, but they pay a lower proportion of their incomes than the poor. This can be seen in Table II (below). *As a percentage of gross income in 2001-2, the poorest group (fifth or quintile) on average paid 41.7% of their incomes in taxes, while the richest fifth (quintile) paid only 34.2%.* This is partly because some very rich people avoid direct taxation by living most of the year outside the country, by the

TABLE II

Taxes as % of Gross Income for all households by quintile groups, 2001-02

Income	% of Gross Income				
Groups	Income tax	All direct taxes	VAT	All indirect taxes	All Taxes
Lowest Fifth	3.2	11.6	11.3	30.1	41.7
2nd fifth	6.3	13.5	7.5	19.9	33.3
3rd fifth	10.3	18.0	7.0	17.7	35.7
4th fifth	13.5	21.2	6.2	15.2	36.4
Top fifth	18.3	23.9	4.6	10.4	34.2

Notes: all direct taxes include Income tax, National Insurance and local taxes
All indirect taxes include VAT, duties on alcohol. tobacco. hydrocarbon oils

Source as for Table I, from Table 3, p.39

use of trusts and other tax havens. Gordon Brown, before New Labour came to power, promised to reduce this massive loss of government revenue, amounting annually to some billions of pounds. Mr Murdoch's newspapers, for example, so it is said, pay no taxes. Apart from this, there are two main reasons for the regressive effect of the tax system. Mrs Thatcher removed the higher rates of income tax on higher incomes and New Labour has not reintroduced them. There is, moreover, no higher rate on national insurance and the extra NI payments to meet the needs of the National Health Service are to be on a flat rate, which will give this tax an even more regressive effect.

The other main reason for the regressive nature of the British tax system is the preponderance of indirect taxes over direct taxes since Mrs Thatcher cut the higher income tax bands and replaced the lost revenue by increasing VAT. New Labour has not changed this. The result can be seen in Table II. *The poorest group pay 30.1% of their gross income in indirect taxes, while the richest pay only 10.4% of theirs. This is an essential part of the silent revolution, in the reverse redistribution of income, which New Labour has not only inherited but also continued.* We don't realise how much we are being taxed when we buy the food and drink and clothing and shoes and fuel that we need. The regressive nature of such indirect taxes becomes obvious, however, when we consider that every household – rich or poor – has to pay the same tax on their purchases. Of course the rich buy more goods and services than the poor, but many of their pleasures – holidays and élite sports abroad such as yachting, boating, golf and tennis – are not taxed.

What has been the effect of New Labour's measures?

Many of New Labour's measures of 'reform' to the tax system have been concerned with getting heads of families and especially single parents back into work. Poor households are caught in what is called the 'poverty trap'. As soon as they begin to earn more they may pay more in tax than the extra income they receive. This is especially true as unemployed people move into employment, and although New Labour's working families tax credits have begun to correct this fault, it has not been totally corrected. The main credits do not go to the poorest groups and especially the women. There are several reasons for this. First, the forms to be filled in so as to make a claim are long and extremely complicated and deter some from applying. Second, partners still receive increased benefit under the scheme when the mother is not working. Most serious is the lack of child care provision and its high cost.

According to a report of the Institute for Fiscal Studies, *Mothers' Employment and Child Care in the UK*, there are eight day nursery places for each 100 children under the age of five, seven child minder places for each 100 children under the age of eight, and six out-of-school club places for each 100 children aged five to seven. According to the same report, working mothers with at least one pre-school child who pay for care, spend on average 13% of their net income on child care. If they are working full time this rises to take a quarter of their net income. No wonder most working mothers going out to work receive care from relatives, friends and neighbours. The effect of the child care subsidies is predicted to raise the employment rate of single mothers by only three percentage points, and to have virtually no impact on the rate for mothers with partners. What has improved the position somewhat in the number of children in poverty under New Labour is not extra government support, but the generally booming economy in the last two decades. The current deepening slump will mean curtains to that.

The conclusion drawn by the most recent June 2003 report of the Institute of Fiscal Studies is that *the total poverty gap – that is the total income by which families fall short of the poverty line – has increased under New Labour.* Living standards for children who were living just below the poverty line in 1996 have improved, but children in families with the lowest incomes have benefited much less. Benefit take-up has been a problem among some of the poorer groups. This is in part because some 600,000 families failed to claim the Working Families Tax Credit – the tax credit aimed at low income families, which was replaced by new tax credits in April 2003. Poverty is a relative concept. As general incomes have risen rapidly in recent years, it has been impossible with current government measures to reduce the number of families and children in poverty, defined as having an income less than 40% of the national average,

Housing costs remain a major cause of poverty. Housing benefit and housing subsidies were once an important element in the Welfare State. An increasingly large contribution to the regressive UK tax system takes place in local government receipts. Mrs Thatcher's poll tax was the most regressive kind of tax ever to be conceived, a tax levied on every household head in the country, with little relation to their income. It aroused so much opposition that it had to be withdrawn. It was replaced by a centrally determined business tax, and by the Council Tax on private dwellings. The latter is still highly regressive, the range of the tax bands on house values being much narrower than the range of incomes on which householders pay income tax. Grants from central government, moreover, which now make up the larger part of local government funding, are based on formulae that are not only very complicated and little understood, but are very far from compensating for low incomes in declining areas of industry.

It is sometimes argued that benefits in kind, not cash, some from local government spending, such as are not included in Table I – housing subsidies, bus and rail subsidies, education, health, etc. – do something to reduce the inequalities in incomes. The figures may be found in the same report on 'The effects of taxes and benefits on household incomes' from which the Table is taken. Farming subsidies are not included in this report.

The effects of the benefits in kind are not impressive. For retired households there is in fact almost no distributive effect from these benefits. This is an important point in view of the widespread belief that rising NHS costs are the result of increased numbers of old people. For non-retired households there are important effects. There is very slightly greater use of the NHS by the poorer groups compared with the richer, presumably because many of the richer make use of private health care.

The biggest difference occurs in the enjoyment of state education, for which the poorest group on average receives nearly five times as much in value as the richest (£3,590 compared with £770). This is firstly because there are three times as many children on average in the bottom quintile of households as in the top quintile, and secondly because three times as many children in the top quintile as in the bottom go to non-state schools. There is a further explanation for the apparent greater use by children in poorer households of the state system in further and higher education, and that is that most children from richer households go to further and higher education away from home, and are thus not counted with their original family household. Size of household is often a factor in determining household income. The middle groups of households have slightly larger numbers, averaging 2.5 persons, whereas 2.3 is the average at both the top and the bottom.

These national figures conceal very big variations in the United Kingdom by region and local areas, in respect of disposable household incomes. (These variations were published in the May 2002 issue of *Economic Trends* as the 'Effects of taxes and benefits on household incomes'.) The variations mainly reflect lower contributions to total UK national income resulting from the rundown of industry, particularly of textiles, mining, heavy engineering and shipbuilding. At the bottom of the Tables, with less than 80% of the national average household income, we find the North and West of Northern Ireland, the Central Valleys of Wales, Hull and East Merseyside. Going up we find East Derbyshire, Nottingham and Leicester with 81%, Sunderland and Powys with 82%, Liverpool with 83%, Gwynedd and West Lothian with 84%. By contrast, West London enjoys 164% of the national average. Broken down to even smaller localities, the variations are even greater, as anyone who has studied the one-time coalfield communities, as Ken Coates and I did (in *Community under Attack*, Spokesman 1997), will have discovered.

A more recent report by a private business intelligence company, CACI, from a postcode survey of household incomes in 2003 showed that inequality was growing between areas. Households in the richest areas were found to have an average annual income six times that of the poorest, and growing in the more prosperous areas around London at double the rate elsewhere. The survey found ten postcode areas with average household annual incomes of over £58,500, and ten with average annual incomes under £13,500. In some rich areas there were incomes of over £100,000 – 18% of households had such incomes in Blackwall ward, Poplar, near Canary Wharf – while in some poor areas there were incomes of under £10,000 – 50% of households had such incomes in St. Helens ward, Middlesborough.

Reversing the Counter-Revolution

The concept of redistribution, that is from the rich to the poor, has been anathema to New Labour. Even the word was avoided as carrying the taint of Old Labour language. In the Autumn of 2002, Mr Blair suddenly began to use the forbidden word. It was not hard to see why. He had to face a critical Trade Union Congress and Labour Party Conference, angry at his expanding use of private capital and private management in the public services, not only of the railways but in education and health, and critical of the all-round, flat-rate increase in national insurance contributions to pay for the NHS, rather than a progressive increase on higher incomes. At the same time, his commitment to the 'blood price' of support for President Bush's war on Iraq was deeply unpopular throughout the Labour Party and the trade unions. 'Redistribution' then looked like a vote winner.

On behalf of the government, however, Lady Hollis made it clear in an interview with Jeremy Paxman ('Newsnight' 19.09.02) that there was no intention of increasing taxation, certainly not of the rich (Lady Hollis should know!), but only of redistributing incomes to target the very poorest. This presumably must mean *within* the bottom quintile. By sticks and carrots the supposedly mulish tendencies of the labour force are to be overcome and more people brought into the labour force. This has been government policy for the last six years and has had no effect in reducing inequalities, for the reasons we have seen – that the tax system is highly regressive. The so-called 'poverty trap' that brings households into tax-paying as soon as they move into paid work has not been eliminated by the tax credit system. With unemployment rising again since mid-2001, and further unemployment predicted for the current recession – not to mention the depressing effects of the Iraq war – such a policy is likely to be even less effective in the future than in the past.

It is far too much to expect that, if the R word (for Redistribution) can now be used again, it might be that the S word (for Socialism) would reappear. This was the stated hope of Roy Hattersley in the interview with Lady Hollis by Jeremy Paxman referred to above. If pigs could fly! Tony Blair will have to go before that could happen, but then so would Gordon Brown, the architect of the latest stage of the silent revolution. As the full impact of this revolution becomes clear – in declining pensions, increasing unemployment, longer hospital queues, larger school classes, soaring house prices, rising crime rates, transport chaos – two societies will emerge: a rich minority who can afford private provision and will resist contributing to a Welfare State, and a poor majority who will find that public services for the poor are poor services. It is a prescription for governments of the right which will respond to every kind of populist, intolerant and xenophobic pressure. It is a nasty prospect. Putting a positive redistribution of incomes once more on the political agenda would mean tackling the culture of greed inaugurated by Mrs Thatcher and extended by New Labour. How could we start to do this?

It is possible that the original income shares of the rich, at least of the very rich, will fall as capital values are reduced in the current slump, though, if unemployment continues to rise, the poorer groups will suffer more. Adjustments in taxation may have to be made by government in such circumstances. Redistribution by the tax system is not a technical question. It is, as I have suggested, a question of power. All sorts of devices seem likely to be introduced by New Labour in relation to pensions and other benefits, which reduce the means of redistribution. Privatisation of public services seems to be set to continue. This has the effect of reducing the services financed by taxation and of increasing the share of private profit. It may be that in future the tax system will not be the best means for redistributing incomes and wealth. There is already much talk of vouchers for health and education and of a capital grant to every new-born child to manage themselves for their education and health and for their protection in case of sickness, unemployment and old age. While children are born into rich or poor homes, whether such schemes benefit the rich or the poor will still depend on the balance of power between capital and labour in determining the size and nature of the grants.

To reduce inequalities, then, it is necessary in a system driven by capital accumulation to devise means for regulating the effects of the working of this system. But what we have seen in the struggle over redistribution is that attempts at regulation are ineffectual when the power of capital is overwhelming. For socialists it is not the effects of income distribution but the system itself that is unacceptable. We are told unceasingly that after the collapse of the Soviet Union there is no alternative. The fact is that there are alternatives, which have not been explored, other than the regimentation of the totalitarian state. The nation state is coming under criticism from the Left and the Right. From the Left, the *Zapatistas'* campaign in Mexico is based on the assumption that revolution today cannot be limited to the capture of the state. An alternative social order has to be built up from the ground. From the Right, we are told that the nation state has already been superseded by the market state. This means that competition in the market increasingly determines the distribution of the resources of each nation as of the whole planet, including capital and incomes. The only possible option is that the market should be freed from all remaining state interference to get on with it. Otherwise, less than optimal production takes place. But in the World Social Forums and elsewhere the question is now being asked whether we need, or can afford for the planet's survival, to encourage unlimited production.

It is noticeable, moreover, that nobody among the ruling élite is proposing the free movement of labour, and there would be much resistance in the United States and in Europe and Japan to the free movement of unsubsidised agricultural products. State protection of national industries is still an important role of the state today. Just listen to President Bush on steel and agricultural protection. The nation state is looked to everywhere by owners of capital to ensure that law and order prevail and that the interests of the largest accumulations of capital are advanced. The fact is that a free market is hardly anywhere to be found where business is not dominated by a small group of large private corporations. Given this fact, it does matter for labour to organise to compete on more equal terms with capital in order to use its power to correct the power already exercised in the market by large scale capital. It has always seemed to follow that labour should seek to use the state to support its efforts.

It may nonetheless be the case that socialists are asking the wrong question today in seeking ways to redistribute incomes within a system of private capitalism. We may have to find a political movement and social commitment that could begin to create a new system, one that does not generate inequality and injustice, not only in individual countries such as Britain but also in the global economy. The task off creating such a system, or perhaps not one but several interlocking systems, is already in progress in the World Social Forum meetings. Solutions are not yet clear, and many alternatives are being discussed, but agreement is unanimous that the present system cannot continue, where inequalities grow ever wider, slumps as well as booms are endemic, and the whole survival of the planet is put at risk by the greed of the rich and by the short-sighted use of resources.

* * *

Also by Michael Barratt Brown

The Third Way ... or Feeding the Fat Cats
ISBN 0 85124 664 8 £2

The Captive Party
How Labour was taken over by Capital
ISBN 0 85124 645 1 £5

* * *

Published in December 2003 by Spokeman Books
for Socialist Renewal,
Russell House, Bulwell Lane, Nottingham, NG6 0BT
phone 0115 970 8318 fax 0115 942 0433
e-mail elfeuro@compuserve.com www.spokesmanbooks.com

ISBN 0851246834

9 780851 246833